PLATO'S
EUTHYDEMUS

Special Edition for Students

PLATO'S EUTHYDEMUS

Translated by:
BENJAMIN JOWETT

Publishers, LLC

ROCKVILLE, MARYLAND
2010

Euthydemus by Plato (Special Edition for Students) in its current format, copyright © Serenity Publishers 2010. This book, in whole or in part, may not be copied or reproduced in its current format by any means, electronic, mechanical or otherwise without the permission of the publisher.

The original text has been reformatted for clarity and to fit this edition.

Serenity Publishers & associated logos are trademarks or registered trademarks of Serenity Publishers, Rockville, Maryland. All other trademarks are properties of their respective owners.

This book is presented as is, without any warranties (implied or otherwise) as to the accuracy of the production, text or translation. The publisher does not take responsibility for any typesetting, formatting, translation or other errors which may have occurred during the production of this book.

ISBN: 978-1-60450-782-9

NOTE FOR TEACHERS

Serenity Publishers can custom create classic texts for your classes

We can create new titles with special pricing and margins

Add your notes and create the book to your exact specifications

Combine different classic texts in one volume

Produce an edition with a special introduction or an afterword

Add your footnotes

Visit **www.SerenityPublishers.com** & **www.ManorStudent.com**
or email **chandi@serenitypublishers.com**

Published by Serenity Publishers
An Arc Manor Company
P. O. Box 10339
Rockville, MD 20849-0339
www.SerenityPublishers.com

Printed in the United States of America/United Kingdom

INTRODUCTION

The Euthydemus, though apt to be regarded by us only as an elaborate jest, has also a very serious purpose. It may fairly claim to be the oldest treatise on logic; for that science originates in the misunderstandings which necessarily accompany the first efforts of speculation. Several of the fallacies which are satirized in it reappear in the Sophistici Elenchi of Aristotle and are retained at the end of our manuals of logic. But if the order of history were followed, they should be placed not at the end but at the beginning of them; for they belong to the age in which the human mind was first making the attempt to distinguish thought from sense, and to separate the universal from the particular or individual. How to put together words or ideas, how to escape ambiguities in the meaning of terms or in the structure of propositions, how to resist the fixed impression of an 'eternal being' or 'perpetual flux,' how to distinguish between words and things—these were problems not easy of solution in the infancy of philosophy. They presented the same kind of difficulty to the half-educated man which spelling or arithmetic do to the mind of a child. It was long before the new world of ideas which had been sought after with such passionate yearning was set in order

Notes

and made ready for use. To us the fallacies which arise in the pre-Socratic philosophy are trivial and obsolete because we are no longer liable to fall into the errors which are expressed by them. The intellectual world has become better assured to us, and we are less likely to be imposed upon by illusions of words.

The logic of Aristotle is for the most part latent in the dialogues of Plato. The nature of definition is explained not by rules but by examples in the Charmides, Lysis, Laches, Protagoras, Meno, Euthyphro, Theaetetus, Gorgias, Republic; the nature of division is likewise illustrated by examples in the Sophist and Statesman; a scheme of categories is found in the Philebus; the true doctrine of contradiction is taught, and the fallacy of arguing in a circle is exposed in the Republic; the nature of synthesis and analysis is graphically described in the Phaedrus; the nature of words is analysed in the Cratylus; the form of the syllogism is indicated in the genealogical trees of the Sophist and Statesman; a true doctrine of predication and an analysis of the sentence are given in the Sophist; the different meanings of one and being are worked out in the Parmenides. Here we have most of the important elements of logic, not yet systematized or reduced to an art or science, but scattered up and down as they would naturally occur in ordinary discourse. They are of little or no use or significance to us; but because we have grown out of the need of them we should not therefore despise them. They are still interesting and instructive for the light which they shed on the history of the human mind.

There are indeed many old fallacies which linger among us, and new ones are constantly springing up. But they are not of the kind to which ancient logic can be usefully applied. The weapons of common sense, not the analytics of Aristotle, are needed for their overthrow. Nor is the use of the Aristotelian logic any longer natural to us. We no longer put arguments into the form of syllogisms like the schoolmen; the simple use of language has been, happily, restored to us. Neither do we discuss the nature of the proposition, nor extract hidden truths from the copula, nor dispute any longer about nominalism and realism. We do not confuse the form with the matter of knowledge, or invent laws of thought, or imagine that any single science furnishes a principle of reasoning to all the rest. Neither do we require categories or heads of argument to be invented for our use. Those who have no knowledge of logic, like some of our great physical philosophers, seem to be quite as good reasoners as those who have. Most of the ancient puzzles have been settled on the basis of usage and common sense; there is no need to reopen them. No science should raise problems or invent forms of thought which add nothing to knowledge and are of no use in assisting the acquisition of it. This seems to be the natural limit of logic and metaphysics; if they give us a more comprehensive or a more definite view of the different spheres of knowledge they are to be studied; if not, not. The better part of ancient logic appears hardly in our own day to have a separate existence; it is absorbed in two other sciences: (1) rhetoric, if indeed this ancient art be not also fading away into literary criticism; (2) the science of language, under which all questions relating to words and propositions and the combinations of them may properly be included.

To continue dead or imaginary sciences, which make no signs of progress and have no definite sphere, tends to interfere with the prosecution of living ones. The study of them is apt to blind the judgment and to render men incapable of seeing the value of evidence, and even of appreciating the nature of truth. Nor should we allow the living science to become confused with the dead by an ambiguity of language. The term logic has two different meanings, an ancient and a modern one, and we vainly try to bridge the gulf between them. Many perplexities are avoided by keeping them apart. There might certainly be a new science of logic; it would not however be built up out of the fragments of the old, but would be distinct from them—relative to the state of knowledge which exists at the present time, and based chiefly on the methods of Modern Inductive philosophy. Such a science might have two legitimate fields: first, the refutation and explanation of false philosophies still hovering in the air as they appear from the point of view of later experience or are comprehended in the history of the human mind, as in a larger horizon: secondly, it might furnish new forms of thought more adequate to the expression of all the diversities and oppositions of knowledge which have grown up in these latter days; it might also suggest new methods of enquiry derived from the comparison of the sciences. Few will deny that the introduction of the words 'subject' and 'object' and the Hegelian reconciliation of opposites have been 'most gracious aids' to psychology, or that the methods of Bacon and Mill have shed a light far and wide on the realms of knowledge. These two great studies, the one destructive and corrective of error, the other conservative and constructive of truth, might be a first and second part of logic. Ancient logic would be the propaedeutic or gate of approach to logical science,—nothing more. But to pursue such speculations further, though not irrelevant, might lead us too far away from the argument of the dialogue.

NOTES

The Euthydemus is, of all the Dialogues of Plato, that in which he approaches most nearly to the comic poet. The mirth is broader, the irony more sustained, the contrast between Socrates and the two Sophists, although veiled, penetrates deeper than in any other of his writings. Even Thrasymachus, in the Republic, is at last pacified, and becomes a friendly and interested auditor of the great discourse. But in the Euthydemus the mask is never dropped; the accustomed irony of Socrates continues to the end...

Socrates narrates to Crito a remarkable scene in which he has himself taken part, and in which the two brothers, Dionysodorus and Euthydemus, are the chief performers. They are natives of Chios, who had settled at Thurii, but were driven out, and in former days had been known at Athens as professors of rhetoric and of the art of fighting in armour. To this they have now added a new accomplishment—the art of Eristic, or fighting with words, which they are likewise willing to teach 'for a consideration.' But they can also teach virtue in a very short time and in the very best manner. Socrates, who is always on the look-out for teachers of virtue, is interested in the youth Cleinias, the grandson of the great Alcibiades, and is desirous that he should have the benefit of their instructions. He is ready to fall down and worship them; although the greatness of their professions does arouse in his mind a temporary incredulity.

A circle gathers round them, in the midst of which are Socrates, the two brothers, the youth Cleinias, who is watched by the eager eyes of his lover Ctesippus, and others. The performance begins; and such a performance as might well seem to require an invocation of Memory and the Muses. It is agreed that the brothers shall question Cleinias. 'Cleinias,' says Euthydemus, 'who learn, the wise

NOTES

or the unwise?' 'The wise,' is the reply; given with blushing and hesitation. 'And yet when you learned you did not know and were not wise.' Then Dionysodorus takes up the ball: 'Who are they who learn dictation of the grammar-master; the wise or the foolish boys?' 'The wise.' 'Then, after all, the wise learn.' 'And do they learn,' said Euthydemus, 'what they know or what they do not know?' 'The latter.' 'And dictation is a dictation of letters?' 'Yes.' 'And you know letters?' 'Yes.' 'Then you learn what you know.' 'But,' retorts Dionysodorus, 'is not learning acquiring knowledge?' 'Yes.' 'And you acquire that which you have not got already?' 'Yes.' 'Then you learn that which you do not know.'

Socrates is afraid that the youth Cleinias may be discouraged at these repeated overthrows. He therefore explains to him the nature of the process to which he is being subjected. The two strangers are not serious; there are jests at the mysteries which precede the enthronement, and he is being initiated into the mysteries of the sophistical ritual. This is all a sort of horse-play, which is now ended. The exhortation to virtue will follow, and Socrates himself (if the wise men will not laugh at him) is desirous of showing the way in which such an exhortation should be carried on, according to his own poor notion. He proceeds to question Cleinias. The result of the investigation may be summed up as follows:—

All men desire good; and good means the possession of goods, such as wealth, health, beauty, birth, power, honour; not forgetting the virtues and wisdom. And yet in this enumeration the greatest good of all is omitted. What is that? Good fortune. But what need is there of good fortune when we have wisdom already:—in every art and business are not the wise also the fortunate? This is admitted. And again, the possession of goods is not enough;

there must also be a right use of them which can only be given by knowledge: in themselves they are neither good nor evil— knowledge and wisdom are the only good, and ignorance and folly the only evil. The conclusion is that we must get 'wisdom.' But can wisdom be taught? 'Yes,' says Cleinias. The ingenuousness of the youth delights Socrates, who is at once relieved from the necessity of discussing one of his great puzzles. 'Since wisdom is the only good, he must become a philosopher, or lover of wisdom.' 'That I will,' says Cleinias.

After Socrates has given this specimen of his own mode of instruction, the two brothers recommence their exhortation to virtue, which is of quite another sort.

'You want Cleinias to be wise?' 'Yes.' 'And he is not wise yet?' 'No.' 'Then you want him to be what he is not, and not to be what he is?—not to be—that is, to perish. Pretty lovers and friends you must all be!'

Here Ctesippus, the lover of Cleinias, interposes in great excitement, thinking that he will teach the two Sophists a lesson of good manners. But he is quickly entangled in the meshes of their sophistry; and as a storm seems to be gathering Socrates pacifies him with a joke, and Ctesippus then says that he is not reviling the two Sophists, he is only contradicting them. 'But,' says Dionysodorus, 'there is no such thing as contradiction. When you and I describe the same thing, or you describe one thing and I describe another, how can there be a contradiction?' Ctesippus is unable to reply.

Socrates has already heard of the denial of contradiction, and would like to be informed by the great master of the art, 'What is the meaning of this paradox? Is there no such thing as error, ignorance,

NOTES

falsehood? Then what are they professing to teach?' The two Sophists complain that Socrates is ready to answer what they said a year ago, but is 'non-plussed' at what they are saying now. 'What does the word "non-plussed" mean?' Socrates is informed, in reply, that words are lifeless things, and lifeless things have no sense or meaning. Ctesippus again breaks out, and again has to be pacified by Socrates, who renews the conversation with Cleinias. The two Sophists are like Proteus in the variety of their transformations, and he, like Menelaus in the Odyssey, hopes to restore them to their natural form.

He had arrived at the conclusion that Cleinias must become a philosopher. And philosophy is the possession of knowledge; and knowledge must be of a kind which is profitable and may be used. What knowledge is there which has such a nature? Not the knowledge which is required in any particular art; nor again the art of the composer of speeches, who knows how to write them, but cannot speak them, although he too must be admitted to be a kind of enchanter of wild animals. Neither is the knowledge which we are seeking the knowledge of the general. For the general makes over his prey to the statesman, as the huntsman does to the cook, or the taker of quails to the keeper of quails; he has not the use of that which he acquires. The two enquirers, Cleinias and Socrates, are described as wandering about in a wilderness, vainly searching after the art of life and happiness. At last they fix upon the kingly art, as having the desired sort of knowledge. But the kingly art only gives men those goods which are neither good nor evil: and if we say further that it makes us wise, in what does it make us wise? Not in special arts, such as cobbling or carpentering, but only in itself: or say again that it makes us good, there is no answer to the question, 'good in what?' At length in despair Cleinias and Socrates turn to the 'Dioscuri' and request their aid.

Euthydemus argues that Socrates knows something; and as he cannot know and not know, he cannot know some things and not know others, and therefore he knows all things: he and Dionysodorus and all other men know all things. 'Do they know shoemaking, etc?' 'Yes.' The sceptical Ctesippus would like to have some evidence of this extraordinary statement: he will believe if Euthydemus will tell him how many teeth Dionysodorus has, and if Dionysodorus will give him a like piece of information about Euthydemus. Even Socrates is incredulous, and indulges in a little raillery at the expense of the brothers. But he restrains himself, remembering that if the men who are to be his teachers think him stupid they will take no pains with him. Another fallacy is produced which turns on the absoluteness of the verb 'to know.' And here Dionysodorus is caught 'napping,' and is induced by Socrates to confess that 'he does not know the good to be unjust.' Socrates appeals to his brother Euthydemus; at the same time he acknowledges that he cannot, like Heracles, fight against a Hydra, and even Heracles, on the approach of a second monster, called upon his nephew Iolaus to help. Dionysodorus rejoins that Iolaus was no more the nephew of Heracles than of Socrates. For a nephew is a nephew, and a brother is a brother, and a father is a father, not of one man only, but of all; nor of men only, but of dogs and sea-monsters. Ctesippus makes merry with the consequences which follow: 'Much good has your father got out of the wisdom of his puppies.'

'But,' says Euthydemus, unabashed, 'nobody wants much good.' Medicine is a good, arms are a good, money is a good, and yet there may be too much of them in wrong places. 'No,' says Ctesippus, 'there cannot be too much gold.' And would you be happy if you had three talents of gold in your belly, a talent in your pate, and a stater in either eye?' Ctesippus, imitating the new wisdom, replies, 'And do not the Scythians reckon those to be the happiest of men who have their skulls gilded and see the inside of them?' 'Do you see,' retorts Euthydemus, 'what has the quality of vision or what has not the quality of vision?' 'What has the quality of vision.' 'And you see our garments?' 'Yes.' 'Then our garments have the quality of vision.' A similar play of words follows, which is successfully retorted by Ctesippus, to the great delight of Cleinias, who is rebuked by Socrates for laughing at such solemn and beautiful things.

'But are there any beautiful things? And if there are such, are they the same or not the same as absolute beauty?' Socrates replies that they are not the same, but each of them has some beauty present with it. 'And are you an ox because you have an ox present with you?' After a few more amphiboliae, in which Socrates, like Ctesippus, in self-defence borrows the weapons of the brothers, they both confess that the two heroes are invincible; and the scene concludes with a grand chorus of shouting and laughing, and a panegyrical oration from Socrates:—

First, he praises the indifference of Dionysodorus and Euthydemus to public opinion; for most persons would rather be refuted by such arguments than use them in the refutation of others. Secondly, he remarks upon their impartiality; for they stop their own mouths, as well as those of other people. Thirdly, he notes their liberality, which makes them give away their secret to all the world: they should be more reserved, and let no one be present at this exhibition who does not pay them a handsome fee; or better still they might practise on one another only. He concludes with a respectful request that they will receive him and Cleinias among their disciples.

Crito tells Socrates that he has heard one of the audience criticise severely this wisdom,—not sparing Socrates himself for countenancing such an exhibition. Socrates asks what manner of man was this censorious critic. 'Not an orator, but a great composer of speeches.' Socrates understands that he is an amphibious animal, half philosopher, half politician; one of a class who have the highest opinion of themselves and a spite against philosophers, whom they imagine to be their rivals. They are a class who are very likely to get mauled by Euthydemus and his friends, and have a great notion of their own wisdom; for they imagine themselves to have all the advantages and none of the drawbacks both of politics and of philosophy. They do not understand the principles of combination, and hence are ignorant that the union of two good things which have different ends produces a compound inferior to either of them taken separately.

Crito is anxious about the education of his children, one of whom is growing up. The description of Dionysodorus and Euthydemus suggests to him the reflection that the professors of education are strange beings. Socrates consoles him with the remark that the good in all professions are few, and recommends that 'he and his house' should continue to serve philosophy, and not mind about its professors.

ooooo

There is a stage in the history of philosophy in which the old is dying out, and the new has not yet come into full life. Great philosophies like the

NOTES

Eleatic or Heraclitean, which have enlarged the boundaries of the human mind, begin to pass away in words. They subsist only as forms which have rooted themselves in language—as troublesome elements of thought which cannot be either used or explained away. The same absoluteness which was once attributed to abstractions is now attached to the words which are the signs of them. The philosophy which in the first and second generation was a great and inspiring effort of reflection, in the third becomes sophistical, verbal, eristic.

It is this stage of philosophy which Plato satirises in the Euthydemus. The fallacies which are noted by him appear trifling to us now, but they were not trifling in the age before logic, in the decline of the earlier Greek philosophies, at a time when language was first beginning to perplex human thought. Besides he is caricaturing them; they probably received more subtle forms at the hands of those who seriously maintained them. They are patent to us in Plato, and we are inclined to wonder how any one could ever have been deceived by them; but we must remember also that there was a time when the human mind was only with great difficulty disentangled from such fallacies.

To appreciate fully the drift of the Euthydemus, we should imagine a mental state in which not individuals only, but whole schools during more than one generation, were animated by the desire to exclude the conception of rest, and therefore the very word 'this' (Theaet.) from language; in which the ideas of space, time, matter, motion, were proved to be contradictory and imaginary; in which the nature of qualitative change was a puzzle, and even differences of degree, when applied to abstract notions, were not understood; in which there was no analysis of grammar, and mere puns or plays of words received serious attention; in which contradiction itself was denied, and, on the one hand, every predicate was affirmed to be true of every subject, and on the other, it was held that no predicate was true of any subject, and that nothing was, or was known, or could be spoken. Let us imagine disputes carried on with religious earnestness and more than scholastic subtlety, in which the catchwords of philosophy are completely detached from their context. (Compare Theaet.) To such disputes the humour, whether of Plato in the ancient, or of Pope and Swift in the modern world, is the natural enemy. Nor must we forget that in modern times also there is no fallacy so gross, no trick of language so transparent, no abstraction so barren and unmeaning, no form of thought so contradictory to experience, which has not been found to satisfy the minds of philosophical enquirers at a certain stage, or when regarded from a certain point of view only. The peculiarity of the fallacies of our own age is that we live within them, and are therefore generally unconscious of them.

Aristotle has analysed several of the same fallacies in his book 'De Sophisticis Elenchis,' which Plato, with equal command of their true nature, has preferred to bring to the test of ridicule. At first we are only struck with the broad humour of this 'reductio ad absurdum:' gradually we perceive that some important questions begin to emerge. Here, as everywhere else, Plato is making war against the philosophers who put words in the place of things, who tear arguments to tatters, who deny predication, and thus make knowledge impossible, to whom ideas and objects of sense have no fixedness, but are in a state of perpetual oscillation and transition. Two great truths seem to be indirectly taught through these fallacies: (1) The uncertainty of language, which allows the same words to be used in different meanings, or with

Notes

different degrees of meaning: (2) The necessary limitation or relative nature of all phenomena. Plato is aware that his own doctrine of ideas, as well as the Eleatic Being and Not-being, alike admit of being regarded as verbal fallacies. The sophism advanced in the Meno, 'that you cannot enquire either into what you know or do not know,' is lightly touched upon at the commencement of the Dialogue; the thesis of Protagoras, that everything is true to him to whom it seems to be true, is satirized. In contrast with these fallacies is maintained the Socratic doctrine that happiness is gained by knowledge. The grammatical puzzles with which the Dialogue concludes probably contain allusions to tricks of language which may have been practised by the disciples of Prodicus or Antisthenes. They would have had more point, if we were acquainted with the writings against which Plato's humour is directed. Most of the jests appear to have a serious meaning; but we have lost the clue to some of them, and cannot determine whether, as in the Cratylus, Plato has or has not mixed up purely unmeaning fun with his satire.

The two discourses of Socrates may be contrasted in several respects with the exhibition of the Sophists: (1) In their perfect relevancy to the subject of discussion, whereas the Sophistical discourses are wholly irrelevant: (2) In their enquiring sympathetic tone, which encourages the youth, instead of 'knocking him down,' after the manner of the two Sophists: (3) In the absence of any definite conclusion—for while Socrates and the youth are agreed that philosophy is to be studied, they are not able to arrive at any certain result about the art which is to teach it. This is a question which will hereafter be answered in the Republic; as the conception of the kingly art is more fully developed in the Politicus, and the caricature of rhetoric in the Gorgias.

The characters of the Dialogue are easily intelligible. There is Socrates once more in the character of an old man; and his equal in years, Crito, the father of Critobulus, like Lysimachus in the Laches, his fellow demesman (Apol.), to whom the scene is narrated, and who once or twice interrupts with a remark after the manner of the interlocutor in the Phaedo, and adds his commentary at the end; Socrates makes a playful allusion to his money-getting habits. There is the youth Cleinias, the grandson of Alcibiades, who may be compared with Lysis, Charmides, Menexenus, and other ingenuous youths out of whose mouths Socrates draws his own lessons, and to whom he always seems to stand in a kindly and sympathetic relation. Crito will not believe that Socrates has not improved or perhaps invented the answers of Cleinias (compare Phaedrus). The name of the grandson of Alcibiades, who is described as long dead, (Greek), and who died at the age of forty-four, in the year 404 B.C., suggests not only that the intended scene of the Euthydemus could not have been earlier than 404, but that as a fact this Dialogue could not have been composed before 390 at the soonest. Ctesippus, who is the lover of Cleinias, has been already introduced to us in the Lysis, and seems there too to deserve the character which is here given him, of a somewhat uproarious young man. But the chief study of all is the picture of the two brothers, who are unapproachable in their effrontery, equally careless of what they say to others and of what is said to them, and never at a loss. They are 'Arcades ambo et cantare pares et respondere parati.' Some superior degree of wit or subtlety is attributed to Euthydemus, who sees the trap in which Socrates catches Dionysodorus.

The epilogue or conclusion of the Dialogue has been criticised as inconsistent with the general

NOTES

scheme. Such a criticism is like similar criticisms on Shakespeare, and proceeds upon a narrow notion of the variety which the Dialogue, like the drama, seems to admit. Plato in the abundance of his dramatic power has chosen to write a play upon a play, just as he often gives us an argument within an argument. At the same time he takes the opportunity of assailing another class of persons who are as alien from the spirit of philosophy as Euthydemus and Dionysodorus. The Eclectic, the Syncretist, the Doctrinaire, have been apt to have a bad name both in ancient and modern times. The persons whom Plato ridicules in the epilogue to the Euthydemus are of this class. They occupy a border-ground between philosophy and politics; they keep out of the dangers of politics, and at the same time use philosophy as a means of serving their own interests. Plato quaintly describes them as making two good things, philosophy and politics, a little worse by perverting the objects of both. Men like Antiphon or Lysias would be types of the class. Out of a regard to the respectabilities of life, they are disposed to censure the interest which Socrates takes in the exhibition of the two brothers. They do not understand, any more than Crito, that he is pursuing his vocation of detecting the follies of mankind, which he finds 'not unpleasant.' (Compare Apol.)

Education is the common subject of all Plato's earlier Dialogues. The concluding remark of Crito, that he has a difficulty in educating his two sons, and the advice of Socrates to him that he should not give up philosophy because he has no faith in philosophers, seems to be a preparation for the more peremptory declaration of the Meno that 'Virtue cannot be taught because there are no teachers.'

The reasons for placing the Euthydemus early in the series are: (1) the similarity in plan and style to the Protagoras, Charmides, and Lysis;—the relation of Socrates to the Sophists is still that of humorous antagonism, not, as in the later Dialogues of Plato, of embittered hatred; and the places and persons have a considerable family likeness; (2) the Euthydemus belongs to the Socratic period in which Socrates is represented as willing to learn, but unable to teach; and in the spirit of Xenophon's Memorabilia, philosophy is defined as 'the knowledge which will make us happy;' (3) we seem to have passed the stage arrived at in the Protagoras, for Socrates is no longer discussing whether virtue can be taught—from this question he is relieved by the ingenuous declaration of the youth Cleinias; and (4) not yet to have reached the point at which he asserts 'that there are no teachers.' Such grounds are precarious, as arguments from style and plan are apt to be (Greek). But no arguments equally strong can be urged in favour of assigning to the Euthydemus any other position in the series.

Euthydemus

PERSONS OF THE DIALOGUE:

*Socrates, who is the narrator of the Dialogue
Crito
Cleinias
Euthydemus
Dionysodorus
Ctesippus*

SCENE:

The Lyceum.

CRITO:

Who was the person, Socrates, with whom you were talking yesterday at the Lyceum? There was such a crowd around you that I could not get within hearing, but I caught a sight of him over their heads, and I made out, as I thought, that he was a stranger with whom you were talking: who was he?

SOCRATES:

There were two, Crito; which of them do you mean?

CRITO:

The one whom I mean was seated second from you on the right-hand side. In the middle was Cleinias the young son of Axiochus, who has wonderfully grown; he is only about the age of my own Critobulus, but he is much forwarder and very good-looking: the other is thin and looks younger than he is.

SOCRATES:

He whom you mean, Crito, is Euthydemus; and on my left hand there was his brother Dionysodorus, who also took part in the conversation.

CRITO:

Neither of them are known to me, Socrates; they are a new importation of Sophists, as I should imagine. Of what country are they, and what is their line of wisdom?

SOCRATES:

As to their origin, I believe that they are natives of this part of the world, and have migrated from Chios to Thurii; they were driven out of Thurii, and have been living for many years past in these regions. As to their wisdom, about which you ask, Crito, they are wonderful— consummate! I never knew what the true pancratiast was before; they are simply made up of fighting, not like the two Acarnanian brothers who fight with their bodies only, but this pair of heroes, besides being perfect in the use of their bodies, are invincible in every sort of warfare; for they are capital at fighting in armour, and will teach the art to any one who pays them; and also they are most skilful in legal warfare; they will plead themselves and teach others to speak and to compose speeches which will have an effect upon the courts. And this was only the beginning of their wisdom, but they have at last carried out the pancratiastic art to the very end, and have mastered the only mode of fighting which had been hitherto neglected by them; and now no one dares even to stand up against them: such is their skill in the war of words, that they can refute any proposition whether true or false. Now I am thinking, Crito, of placing myself in their hands; for they say that in a short time they can impart their skill to any one.

CRITO:

But, Socrates, are you not too old? there may be reason to fear that.

SOCRATES:

Certainly not, Crito; as I will prove to you, for I have the consolation of knowing that they began this art of disputation which I covet, quite, as I may say, in old age; last year, or the year before, they had none of their new wisdom. I am only apprehensive that I may bring the two strangers into disrepute, as I have done Connus the son of Metrobius, the harp-player, who is still my music-master; for when the boys who go to him see me going with them, they laugh at me and call him grandpapa's master. Now I should not like the strangers to experience similar treatment; the fear of ridicule may make them unwilling to receive me; and therefore, Crito, I shall try and persuade some old men to accompany me to them, as I persuaded them to go with me to Connus, and I hope that you will make one: and perhaps we had better take your sons as a bait; they will want to have them as pupils, and for the sake of them willing to receive us.

CRITO:

I see no objection, Socrates, if you like; but first I wish that you would give me a description of their wisdom, that I may know beforehand what we are going to learn.

SOCRATES:

In less than no time you shall hear; for I cannot say that I did not attend—I paid great attention to them, and I remember and will endeavour to repeat the whole story. Providentially I was sitting alone in the dressing-room of the Lyceum where you saw me, and was about to depart; when I was getting up I recognized the familiar divine sign: so I sat down again, and in a little while the two brothers Euthydemus and Dionysodorus came in, and several others with them, whom I believe to be their disciples, and they walked about in the covered court; they had not taken more than two or three turns when Cleinias entered, who, as you truly say, is very much improved: he was followed by a host of lovers, one of whom was Ctesippus the Paeanian, a well-bred youth, but also having the wildness of youth. Cleinias saw me from the entrance as I was sitting alone, and at once came and sat down on the right hand of me, as you describe; and Dionysodorus and Euthydemus, when they saw him, at first stopped and talked with one another, now and then glancing at us, for I particularly watched them; and then Euthydemus came and sat down by the youth, and the other by me on the left hand; the rest anywhere. I saluted the brothers, whom I had not seen for a long time; and then I said to Cleinias: Here are two wise men, Euthydemus and Dionysodorus, Cleinias, wise not in a small but in a large way of wisdom, for they know all about war,—all that a good general ought to know about the array and command of an army, and the whole art of fighting in armour: and they know about law too, and can teach a man how to use the weapons of the courts when he is injured.

They heard me say this, but only despised me. I observed that they looked at one another, and both of them laughed; and then Euthydemus said: Those, Socrates, are matters which we no longer pursue seriously; to us they are secondary occupations.

Indeed, I said, if such occupations are regarded by you as secondary, what must the principal one be; tell me, I beseech you, what that noble study is?

The teaching of virtue, Socrates, he replied, is our principal occupation; and we believe that we can impart it better and quicker than any man.

My God! I said, and where did you learn that? I always thought, as I was saying just now, that your chief accomplishment was the art of fighting in armour; and I used to say as much of you, for I remember that you professed this when you were here before. But now if you really have the other knowledge, O forgive me: I address you as I would superior beings, and ask you to pardon the impiety of my former expressions. But are you quite sure about this, Dionysodorus and Euthydemus? the promise is so vast, that a feeling of incredulity steals over me.

You may take our word, Socrates, for the fact.

Then I think you happier in having such a treasure than the great king is in the possession of his kingdom. And please to tell me whether you intend to exhibit your wisdom; or what will you do?

That is why we have come hither, Socrates; and our purpose is not only to exhibit, but also to teach any one who likes to learn.

But I can promise you, I said, that every unvirtuous person will want to learn. I shall be the first; and there is the youth Cleinias, and Ctesippus: and here are several others, I said, pointing to the lovers of Cleinias, who were beginning to gather round us. Now Ctesippus was sitting at some distance from Cleinias; and when Euthydemus leaned forward in talking with me, he was prevented from seeing Cleinias, who was between us; and so, partly because he wanted to look at his love, and also because he was interested, he jumped up and stood opposite to us: and all the other admirers of Cleinias, as well as the disciples of Euthydemus and Dionysodorus, followed his example. And these were the persons whom I showed to Euthydemus, telling him that they were all eager to learn: to which Ctesippus and all of them with one voice vehemently assented, and bid him exhibit the power of his wisdom. Then I said: O Euthydemus and Dionysodorus, I earnestly request you to do myself and the company the favour to exhibit. There may be some trouble in giving the whole exhibition; but tell me one thing,—can you make a good man of him only who is already convinced that he ought to learn of you, or of him also who is not convinced, either because he imagines that virtue is a thing which cannot be taught at all, or that you are not the teachers of it? Has your art power to persuade him, who is of the latter temper of mind, that virtue can be taught; and that you are the men from whom he will best learn it?

Certainly, Socrates, said Dionysodorus; our art will do both.

And you and your brother, Dionysodorus, I said, of all men who are now living are the most likely to stimulate him to philosophy and to the study of virtue?

Yes, Socrates, I rather think that we are.

Then I wish that you would be so good as to defer the other part of the exhibition, and only try to persuade the youth whom you see here that he ought to be a philosopher and study virtue. Exhibit that, and you will confer a great favour on me and on every one present; for the fact is I and all of us are extremely anxious that he should become truly good. His name is Cleinias, and he is the son of Axiochus, and grandson of the old Alcibiades, cousin of the Alcibiades that now is. He is quite young, and we are naturally afraid that some one may get the start of us, and turn his mind in a wrong direction, and he may be ruined. Your visit, therefore, is most happily timed; and I hope that you will make a trial of the young man, and converse with him in our presence, if you have no objection.

These were pretty nearly the expressions which I used; and Euthydemus, in a manly and at the same time encouraging tone, replied: There can be no objection, Socrates, if the young man is only willing to answer questions.

He is quite accustomed to do so, I replied; for his friends often come and ask him questions and argue with him; and therefore he is quite at home in answering.

What followed, Crito, how can I rightly narrate? For not slight is the task of rehearsing infinite wisdom, and therefore, like the poets, I ought to commence my relation with an invocation to Memory and the Muses. Now Euthydemus, if I remember rightly, began nearly as follows: O Cleinias, are those who learn the wise or the ignorant?

The youth, overpowered by the question blushed, and in his perplexity looked at me for help; and

I, knowing that he was disconcerted, said: Take courage, Cleinias, and answer like a man whichever you think; for my belief is that you will derive the greatest benefit from their questions.

Whichever he answers, said Dionysodorus, leaning forward so as to catch my ear, his face beaming with laughter, I prophesy that he will be refuted, Socrates.

While he was speaking to me, Cleinias gave his answer: and therefore I had no time to warn him of the predicament in which he was placed, and he answered that those who learned were the wise.

Euthydemus proceeded: There are some whom you would call teachers, are there not?

The boy assented.

And they are the teachers of those who learn—the grammar-master and the lyre-master used to teach you and other boys; and you were the learners?

Yes.

And when you were learners you did not as yet know the things which you were learning?

No, he said.

And were you wise then?

No, indeed, he said.

But if you were not wise you were unlearned?

Certainly.

You then, learning what you did not know, were unlearned when you were learning?

The youth nodded assent.

Then the unlearned learn, and not the wise, Cleinias, as you imagine.

At these words the followers of Euthydemus, of whom I spoke, like a chorus at the bidding of their director, laughed and cheered. Then, before the youth had time to recover his breath, Dionysodorus cleverly took him in hand, and said: Yes, Cleinias; and when the grammar-master dictated anything to you, were they the wise boys or the unlearned who learned the dictation?

The wise, replied Cleinias.

Then after all the wise are the learners and not the unlearned; and your last answer to Euthydemus was wrong.

Then once more the admirers of the two heroes, in an ecstasy at their wisdom, gave vent to another peal of laughter, while the rest of us were silent and amazed. Euthydemus, observing this, determined to persevere with the youth; and in order to heighten the effect went on asking another similar question, which might be compared to the double turn of an expert dancer. Do those, said he, who learn, learn what they know, or what they do not know?

Again Dionysodorus whispered to me: That, Socrates, is just another of the same sort.

Good heavens, I said; and your last question was so good!

Like all our other questions, Socrates, he replied—inevitable.

I see the reason, I said, why you are in such reputation among your disciples.

Meanwhile Cleinias had answered Euthydemus that those who learned learn what they do not know; and he put him through a series of questions the same as before.

Do you not know letters?

He assented.

All letters?

Yes.

But when the teacher dictates to you, does he not dictate letters?

To this also he assented.

Then if you know all letters, he dictates that which you know?

This again was admitted by him.

Then, said the other, you do not learn that which he dictates; but he only who does not know letters learns?

Nay, said Cleinias; but I do learn.

Then, said he, you learn what you know, if you know all the letters?

He admitted that.

Then, he said, you were wrong in your answer.

The word was hardly out of his mouth when Dionysodorus took up the argument, like a ball which he caught, and had another throw at the youth. Cleinias, he said, Euthydemus is deceiving you. For tell me now, is not learning acquiring knowledge of that which one learns?

Cleinias assented.

And knowing is having knowledge at the time?

He agreed.

And not knowing is not having knowledge at the time?

He admitted that.

And are those who acquire those who have or have not a thing?

Those who have not.

And have you not admitted that those who do not know are of the number of those who have not?

He nodded assent.

Then those who learn are of the class of those who acquire, and not of those who have?

He agreed.

Then, Cleinias, he said, those who do not know learn, and not those who know.

Euthydemus was proceeding to give the youth a third fall; but I knew that he was in deep water, and therefore, as I wanted to give him a respite lest he should be disheartened, I said to him consolingly: You must not be surprised, Cleinias, at the singularity of their mode of speech: this I say because you may not understand what the two strangers are doing with you; they are only initiating you after the manner of the Corybantes in the mysteries; and this answers to the enthronement, which, if you have ever been initiated, is, as you will know, accompanied by dancing and sport; and now they are just prancing and dancing about you, and will next proceed to initiate you; imagine then that you have gone through the first part of the sophistical ritual, which, as Prodicus says, begins with initiation into the correct use of terms. The two foreign gentlemen, perceiving that you did not know, wanted to explain to you that the word 'to learn' has two meanings, and is used, first, in the sense of acquiring knowledge of some matter of which you previously have no knowledge, and also, when you have the knowledge, in the sense of reviewing this matter, whether something done or spoken by the light of this newly-acquired knowledge; the latter is generally called 'knowing' rather than 'learning,' but the word 'learning' is also used; and you did not see, as they explained to you, that the term is employed of two opposite sorts of men, of those who know, and of those who do not know. There was a similar trick in the second question, when they asked you whether men learn what they know or what they do not know. These parts of learning are not serious, and therefore I say that the gentlemen are not serious, but are only playing with you. For if a man had all that sort of knowledge that ever was, he would not be at all the wiser; he would only be able to play with men, tripping them up and oversetting them with distinctions of words. He would be like a person who pulls away a stool from some one when he is about to sit down, and then laughs and makes merry at the sight of his friend overturned and laid on his back. And you must regard all that has hitherto passed between you and them as merely play. But in what is to follow I am certain that they will exhibit to you their serious purpose, and keep their promise (I will show them how); for they promised to give me a sample of the hortatory philosophy, but I suppose that they wanted to have a game with you first. And now, Euthydemus and Dionysodorus, I think that we have had enough of this. Will you let me see you explaining to the young man how he is to apply himself to the study of virtue and wisdom?

And I will first show you what I conceive to be the nature of the task, and what sort of a discourse I desire to hear; and if I do this in a very inartistic and ridiculous manner, do not laugh at me, for I only venture to improvise before you because I am eager to hear your wisdom: and I must therefore ask you and your disciples to refrain from laughing. And now, O son of Axiochus, let me put a question to you: Do not all men desire happiness? And yet, perhaps, this is one of those ridiculous questions which I am afraid to ask, and which ought not to be asked by a sensible man: for what human being is there who does not desire happiness?

There is no one, said Cleinias, who does not.

Well, then, I said, since we all of us desire happiness, how can we be happy?—that is the next question. Shall we not be happy if we have many good things? And this, perhaps, is even a more simple question than the first, for there can be no doubt of the answer.

He assented.

And what things do we esteem good? No solemn sage is required to tell us this, which may be easily answered; for every one will say that wealth is a good.

Certainly, he said.

And are not health and beauty goods, and other personal gifts?

He agreed.

Can there be any doubt that good birth, and power, and honours in one's own land, are goods?

He assented.

And what other goods are there? I said. What do you say of temperance, justice, courage: do you not verily and indeed think, Cleinias, that we shall be more right in ranking them as goods than in not ranking them as goods? For a dispute might possibly arise about this. What then do you say?

They are goods, said Cleinias.

Very well, I said; and where in the company shall we find a place for wisdom—among the goods or not?

Among the goods.

And now, I said, think whether we have left out any considerable goods.

I do not think that we have, said Cleinias.

Upon recollection, I said, indeed I am afraid that we have left out the greatest of them all.

What is that? he asked.

Fortune, Cleinias, I replied; which all, even the most foolish, admit to be the greatest of goods.

True, he said.

On second thoughts, I added, how narrowly, O son of Axiochus, have you and I escaped making a laughing-stock of ourselves to the strangers.

Why do you say so?

Why, because we have already spoken of good-fortune, and are but repeating ourselves.

What do you mean?

I mean that there is something ridiculous in again putting forward good-fortune, which has a place in the list already, and saying the same thing twice over.

He asked what was the meaning of this, and I replied: Surely wisdom is good-fortune; even a child may know that.

The simple-minded youth was amazed; and, observing his surprise, I said to him: Do you not know, Cleinias, that flute-players are most fortunate and successful in performing on the flute?

He assented.

And are not the scribes most fortunate in writing and reading letters?

Certainly.

Amid the dangers of the sea, again, are any more fortunate on the whole than wise pilots?

None, certainly.

And if you were engaged in war, in whose company would you rather take the risk—in company with a wise general, or with a foolish one?

With a wise one.

And if you were ill, whom would you rather have as a companion in a dangerous illness—a wise physician, or an ignorant one?

A wise one.

You think, I said, that to act with a wise man is more fortunate than to act with an ignorant one?

He assented.

Then wisdom always makes men fortunate: for by wisdom no man would ever err, and therefore he must act rightly and succeed, or his wisdom would be wisdom no longer.

We contrived at last, somehow or other, to agree in a general conclusion, that he who had wisdom had no need of fortune. I then recalled to his mind the previous state of the question. You remember, I said, our making the admission that we should be happy and fortunate if many good things were present with us?

He assented.

And should we be happy by reason of the presence of good things, if they profited us not, or if they profited us?

If they profited us, he said.

And would they profit us, if we only had them and did not use them? For example, if we had a great deal of food and did not eat, or a great deal of drink and did not drink, should we be profited?

Certainly not, he said.

Or would an artisan, who had all the implements necessary for his work, and did not use them, be any the better for the possession of them? For example, would a carpenter be any the better for having all his tools and plenty of wood, if he never worked?

Certainly not, he said.

And if a person had wealth and all the goods of which we were just now speaking, and did not use them, would he be happy because he possessed them?

No indeed, Socrates.

Then, I said, a man who would be happy must not only have the good things, but he must also use them; there is no advantage in merely having them?

True.

Well, Cleinias, but if you have the use as well as the possession of good things, is that sufficient to confer happiness?

Yes, in my opinion.

And may a person use them either rightly or wrongly?

He must use them rightly.

That is quite true, I said. And the wrong use of a thing is far worse than the non-use; for the one is an evil, and the other is neither a good nor an evil. You admit that?

He assented.

Now in the working and use of wood, is not that which gives the right use simply the knowledge of the carpenter?

Nothing else, he said.

And surely, in the manufacture of vessels, knowledge is that which gives the right way of making them?

He agreed.

And in the use of the goods of which we spoke at first—wealth and health and beauty, is not knowledge that which directs us to the right use of them, and regulates our practice about them?

He assented.

Then in every possession and every use of a thing, knowledge is that which gives a man not only good-fortune but success?

He again assented.

And tell me, I said, O tell me, what do possessions profit a man, if he have neither good sense nor wisdom? Would a man be better off, having and doing many things without wisdom, or a few things with wisdom? Look at the matter thus: If he did fewer things would he not make fewer mistakes? if he made fewer mistakes would he not have fewer misfortunes? and if he had fewer misfortunes would he not be less miserable?

Certainly, he said.

And who would do least—a poor man or a rich man?

A poor man.

A weak man or a strong man?

A weak man.

A noble man or a mean man?

A mean man.

And a coward would do less than a courageous and temperate man?

Yes.

And an indolent man less than an active man?

He assented.

And a slow man less than a quick; and one who had dull perceptions of seeing and hearing less than one who had keen ones?

All this was mutually allowed by us.

Then, I said, Cleinias, the sum of the matter appears to be that the goods of which we spoke before are not to be regarded as goods in themselves, but the degree of good and evil in them depends on whether they are or are not under the guidance of knowledge: under the guidance of ignorance, they are greater evils than their opposites, inasmuch as they are more able to minister to the evil principle which rules them; and when under the guidance of wisdom and prudence, they are greater goods: but in themselves they are nothing?

That, he replied, is obvious.

What then is the result of what has been said? Is not this the result— that other things are indifferent, and that wisdom is the only good, and ignorance the only evil?

He assented.

Let us consider a further point, I said: Seeing that all men desire happiness, and happiness, as has been shown, is gained by a use, and a right use, of the things of life, and the right use of them, and good-fortune in the use of them, is given by knowledge,—the inference is that everybody ought by all means to try and make himself as wise as he can?

Yes, he said.

And when a man thinks that he ought to obtain this treasure, far more than money, from a father or a guardian or a friend or a suitor, whether citizen or stranger—the eager desire and prayer to them that they would impart wisdom to you, is not at all dishonourable, Cleinias; nor is any one to be blamed for doing any honourable service or ministration to any man, whether a lover or not, if his aim is to get wisdom. Do you agree? I said.

Yes, he said, I quite agree, and think that you are right.

Yes, I said, Cleinias, if only wisdom can be taught, and does not come to man spontaneously; for this is a point which has still to be considered, and is not yet agreed upon by you and me—

But I think, Socrates, that wisdom can be taught, he said.

Best of men, I said, I am delighted to hear you say so; and I am also grateful to you for having saved me from a long and tiresome investigation as to whether wisdom can be taught or not. But now, as you think that wisdom can be taught, and that wisdom only can make a man happy and fortunate, will you not acknowledge that all of us ought to love wisdom, and you individually will try to love her?

Certainly, Socrates, he said; I will do my best.

I was pleased at hearing this; and I turned to Dionysodorus and Euthydemus and said: That is an example, clumsy and tedious I admit, of the sort of exhortations which I would have you give; and I hope that one of you will set forth what I have been saying in a more artistic style: or at least take up the enquiry where I left off, and proceed to show the youth whether he should have all knowledge; or whether there is one sort of knowledge only which will make him good and happy, and what that is. For, as I was saying at first, the improvement of this young man in virtue and wisdom is a matter which we have very much at heart.

Thus I spoke, Crito, and was all attention to what was coming. I wanted to see how they would approach the question, and where they would start in their exhortation to the young man that he should practise wisdom and virtue. Dionysodorus, who was the elder, spoke first. Everybody's eyes were directed towards him, perceiving that something wonderful might shortly be expected. And certainly they were not far wrong; for the man, Crito, began a remarkable discourse well worth hearing, and wonderfully persuasive regarded as an exhortation to virtue.

Tell me, he said, Socrates and the rest of you who say that you want this young man to become wise, are you in jest or in real earnest?

I was led by this to imagine that they fancied us to have been jesting when we asked them to converse with the youth, and that this made them jest and play, and being under this impression, I was the more decided in saying that we were in profound earnest. Dionysodorus said:

Reflect, Socrates; you may have to deny your words.

I have reflected, I said; and I shall never deny my words.

Well, said he, and so you say that you wish Cleinias to become wise?

Undoubtedly.

And he is not wise as yet?

At least his modesty will not allow him to say that he is.

You wish him, he said, to become wise and not, to be ignorant?

That we do.

You wish him to be what he is not, and no longer to be what he is?

I was thrown into consternation at this.

Taking advantage of my consternation he added: You wish him no longer to be what he is, which can only mean that you wish him to perish. Pretty lovers and friends they must be who want their favourite not to be, or to perish!

When Ctesippus heard this he got very angry (as a lover well might) and said: Stranger of Thurii—if politeness would allow me I should say, A plague upon you! What can make you tell such a lie about me and the others, which I hardly like to repeat, as that I wish Cleinias to perish?

Euthydemus replied: And do you think, Ctesippus, that it is possible to tell a lie?

Yes, said Ctesippus; I should be mad to say anything else.

And in telling a lie, do you tell the thing of which you speak or not?

You tell the thing of which you speak.

And he who tells, tells that thing which he tells, and no other?

Yes, said Ctesippus.

And that is a distinct thing apart from other things?

Certainly.

And he who says that thing says that which is?

Yes.

And he who says that which is, says the truth. And therefore Dionysodorus, if he says that which is, says the truth of you and no lie.

Yes, Euthydemus, said Ctesippus; but in saying this, he says what is not.

Euthydemus answered: And that which is not is not?

True.

And that which is not is nowhere?

Nowhere.

And can any one do anything about that which has no existence, or do to Cleinias that which is not and is nowhere?

I think not, said Ctesippus.

Well, but do rhetoricians, when they speak in the assembly, do nothing?

Nay, he said, they do something.

And doing is making?

Yes.

And speaking is doing and making?

He agreed.

Then no one says that which is not, for in saying what is not he would be doing something; and you have already acknowledged that no one can do what is not. And therefore, upon your own showing, no one says what is false; but if Dionysodorus says anything, he says what is true and what is.

Yes, Euthydemus, said Ctesippus; but he speaks of things in a certain way and manner, and not as they really are.

Why, Ctesippus, said Dionysodorus, do you mean to say that any one speaks of things as they are?

Yes, he said—all gentlemen and truth-speaking persons.

And are not good things good, and evil things evil?

He assented.

And you say that gentlemen speak of things as they are?

Yes.

Then the good speak evil of evil things, if they speak of them as they are?

Yes, indeed, he said; and they speak evil of evil men. And if I may give you a piece of advice, you had better take care that they do not speak evil of you, since I can tell you that the good speak evil of the evil.

And do they speak great things of the great, rejoined Euthydemus, and warm things of the warm?

To be sure they do, said Ctesippus; and they speak coldly of the insipid and cold dialectician.

You are abusive, Ctesippus, said Dionysodorus, you are abusive!

Indeed, I am not, Dionysodorus, he replied; for I love you and am giving you friendly advice, and, if I could, would persuade you not like a boor to say in my presence that I desire my beloved, whom I value above all men, to perish.

I saw that they were getting exasperated with one another, so I made a joke with him and said: O Ctesippus, I think that we must allow the strangers to use language in their own way, and not quarrel with them about words, but be thankful for what they give us. If they know how to destroy men in such a way as to make good and sensible men out of bad and foolish ones— whether this is a discovery of their own, or whether they have learned from some one else this new sort of death and destruction which enables them to get rid of a bad man and turn him into a good one—if they know this (and they do know this—at any rate they said just now that this was the secret of their newly-discovered art)—let them, in their phraseology, destroy the youth and make him wise, and all of us with him. But if you young men do not like to trust yourselves with them, then fiat experimentum in corpore senis; I will be the Carian on whom they shall operate. And here I offer my old person to Dionysodorus; he may put me into the pot, like Medea the Colchian, kill me, boil me, if he will only make me good.

Ctesippus said: And I, Socrates, am ready to commit myself to the strangers; they may skin me alive, if they please (and I am pretty well skinned by them already), if only my skin is made at last, not like that of Marsyas, into a leathern bottle, but into a piece of virtue. And here is Dionysodorus fancying that I am angry with him, when really I am not angry at all; I do but contradict him when I think that he is speaking improperly to me: and you must not confound abuse and contradiction, O illustrious Dionysodorus; for they are quite different things.

Contradiction! said Dionysodorus; why, there never was such a thing.

Certainly there is, he replied; there can be no question of that. Do you, Dionysodorus, maintain that there is not?

You will never prove to me, he said, that you have heard any one contradicting any one else.

Indeed, said Ctesippus; then now you may hear me contradicting Dionysodorus.

Are you prepared to make that good?

Certainly, he said.

Well, have not all things words expressive of them?

Yes.

Of their existence or of their non-existence?

Of their existence.

Yes, Ctesippus, and we just now proved, as you may remember, that no man could affirm a negative; for no one could affirm that which is not.

And what does that signify? said Ctesippus; you and I may contradict all the same for that.

But can we contradict one another, said Dionysodorus, when both of us are describing the same thing? Then we must surely be speaking the same thing?

He assented.

Or when neither of us is speaking of the same thing? For then neither of us says a word about the thing at all?

He granted that proposition also.

But when I describe something and you describe another thing, or I say something and you say nothing—is there any contradiction? How can he who speaks contradict him who speaks not?

Here Ctesippus was silent; and I in my astonishment said: What do you mean, Dionysodorus? I have often heard, and have been amazed to hear, this thesis of yours, which is maintained and employed by the disciples of Protagoras, and others before them, and which to me appears to be quite wonderful, and suicidal as well as destructive, and I think that I am most likely to hear the truth about it from you. The dictum is that there is no such thing as falsehood; a man must either say what is true or say nothing. Is not that your position?

He assented.

But if he cannot speak falsely, may he not think falsely?

No, he cannot, he said.

Then there is no such thing as false opinion?

No, he said.

Then there is no such thing as ignorance, or men who are ignorant; for is not ignorance, if there be such a thing, a mistake of fact?

Certainly, he said.

And that is impossible?

Impossible, he replied.

Are you saying this as a paradox, Dionysodorus; or do you seriously maintain no man to be ignorant?

Refute me, he said.

But how can I refute you, if, as you say, to tell a falsehood is impossible?

Very true, said Euthydemus.

Neither did I tell you just now to refute me, said Dionysodorus; for how can I tell you to do that which is not?

O Euthydemus, I said, I have but a dull conception of these subtleties and excellent devices of wisdom;

I am afraid that I hardly understand them, and you must forgive me therefore if I ask a very stupid question: if there be no falsehood or false opinion or ignorance, there can be no such thing as erroneous action, for a man cannot fail of acting as he is acting—that is what you mean?

Yes, he replied.

And now, I said, I will ask my stupid question: If there is no such thing as error in deed, word, or thought, then what, in the name of goodness, do you come hither to teach? And were you not just now saying that you could teach virtue best of all men, to any one who was willing to learn?

And are you such an old fool, Socrates, rejoined Dionysodorus, that you bring up now what I said at first—and if I had said anything last year, I suppose that you would bring that up too—but are nonplussed at the words which I have just uttered?

Why, I said, they are not easy to answer; for they are the words of wise men: and indeed I know not what to make of this word 'nonplussed,' which you used last: what do you mean by it, Dionysodorus? You must mean that I cannot refute your argument. Tell me if the words have any other sense.

No, he replied, they mean what you say. And now answer.

What, before you, Dionysodorus? I said.

Answer, said he.

And is that fair?

Yes, quite fair, he said.

Upon what principle? I said. I can only suppose that you are a very wise man who comes to us in the character of a great logician, and who knows when to answer and when not to answer—and now you will not open your mouth at all, because you know that you ought not.

You prate, he said, instead of answering. But if, my good sir, you admit that I am wise, answer as I tell you.

I suppose that I must obey, for you are master. Put the question.

Are the things which have sense alive or lifeless?

They are alive.

And do you know of any word which is alive?

I cannot say that I do.

Then why did you ask me what sense my words had?

Why, because I was stupid and made a mistake. And yet, perhaps, I was right after all in saying that words have a sense;—what do you say, wise man? If I was not in error, even you will not refute me, and all your wisdom will be non-plussed; but if I did fall into error, then again you are wrong in saying that there is no error,—and this remark was made by you not quite a year ago. I am inclined to think, however, Dionysodorus and Euthydemus, that this argument lies where it was and is not very likely to advance: even your skill in the subtleties of logic, which is really amazing, has not found out the way of throwing another and not falling yourself, now any more than of old.

Ctesippus said: Men of Chios, Thurii, or however and whatever you call yourselves, I wonder at you, for you seem to have no objection to talking nonsense.

Fearing that there would be high words, I again endeavoured to soothe Ctesippus, and said to him: To you, Ctesippus, I must repeat what I said before to Cleinias—that you do not understand the ways of these philosophers from abroad. They are not serious, but, like the Egyptian wizard, Proteus, they take different forms and deceive us by their enchantments: and let us, like Menelaus, refuse to let them go until they show themselves to us in earnest. When they begin to be in earnest their full beauty will appear: let us then beg and entreat and beseech them to shine forth. And I think that I had better once more exhibit the form in which I pray to behold them; it might be a guide to them. I will go on therefore where I left off, as well as I can, in the hope that I may touch their hearts and move them to pity, and that when they see me deeply serious and interested, they also may be serious. You, Cleinias, I said, shall remind me at what point we left off. Did we not agree that philosophy should be studied? and was not that our conclusion?

Yes, he replied.

And philosophy is the acquisition of knowledge?

Yes, he said.

And what knowledge ought we to acquire? May we not answer with absolute truth—A knowledge which will do us good?

Certainly, he said.

And should we be any the better if we went about having a knowledge of the places where most gold was hidden in the earth?

Perhaps we should, he said.

But have we not already proved, I said, that we should be none the better off, even if without trouble and digging all the gold which there is in the earth were ours? And if we knew how to convert stones into gold, the knowledge would be of no value to us, unless we also knew how to use the gold? Do you not remember? I said.

I quite remember, he said.

Nor would any other knowledge, whether of money-making, or of medicine, or of any other art which knows only how to make a thing, and not to use it when made, be of any good to us. Am I not right?

He agreed.

And if there were a knowledge which was able to make men immortal, without giving them the knowledge of the way to use the immortality, neither would there be any use in that, if we may argue from the analogy of the previous instances?

To all this he agreed.

Then, my dear boy, I said, the knowledge which we want is one that uses as well as makes?

True, he said.

And our desire is not to be skilful lyre-makers, or artists of that sort— far otherwise; for with them the art which makes is one, and the art which uses is another. Although they have to do with the same, they are divided: for the art which makes and the art which plays on the lyre differ widely from one another. Am I not right?

He agreed.

And clearly we do not want the art of the flute-maker; this is only another of the same sort?

He assented.

But suppose, I said, that we were to learn the art of making speeches— would that be the art which would make us happy?

I should say, no, rejoined Cleinias.

And why should you say so? I asked.

I see, he replied, that there are some composers of speeches who do not know how to use the speeches which they make, just as the makers of lyres do not know how to use the lyres; and also some who are of themselves unable to compose speeches, but are able to use the speeches which the others make for them; and this proves that the art of making speeches is not the same as the art of using them.

Yes, I said; and I take your words to be a sufficient proof that the art of making speeches is not one which will make a man happy. And yet I did think that the art which we have so long been seeking might be discovered in that direction; for the composers of speeches, whenever I meet them, always appear to me to be very extraordinary men, Cleinias, and their art is lofty and divine, and no wonder. For their art is a part of the great art of enchantment, and hardly, if at all, inferior to it: and whereas the art of the enchanter is a mode of charming snakes and spiders and scorpions, and other monsters and pests, this art of their's acts upon dicasts and ecclesiasts and bodies of men, for the charming and pacifying of them. Do you agree with me?

Yes, he said, I think that you are quite right.

Whither then shall we go, I said, and to what art shall we have recourse?

I do not see my way, he said.

But I think that I do, I replied.

And what is your notion? asked Cleinias.

I think that the art of the general is above all others the one of which the possession is most likely to make a man happy.

I do not think so, he said.

Why not? I said.

The art of the general is surely an art of hunting mankind.

What of that? I said.

Why, he said, no art of hunting extends beyond hunting and capturing; and when the prey is taken the huntsman or fisherman cannot use it; but they hand it over to the cook, and the geometricians and astronomers and calculators (who all belong to the hunting class, for they do not make their diagrams, but only find out that which was previously contained in them)—they, I say, not being able to use but only to catch their prey, hand over their inventions to the dialectician to be applied by him, if they have any sense in them.

Good, I said, fairest and wisest Cleinias. And is this true?

Certainly, he said; just as a general when he takes a city or a camp hands over his new acquisition to the statesman, for he does not know how to use them himself; or as the quail-taker transfers the quails to the keeper of them. If we are looking for the art which is to make us blessed, and which is able to use that which it makes or takes, the art of the general is not the one, and some other must be found.

CRITO:

And do you mean, Socrates, that the youngster said all this?

SOCRATES:

Are you incredulous, Crito?

CRITO:

Indeed, I am; for if he did say so, then in my opinion he needs neither Euthydemus nor any one else to be his instructor.

SOCRATES:

Perhaps I may have forgotten, and Ctesippus was the real answerer.

CRITO:

Ctesippus! nonsense.

SOCRATES:

All I know is that I heard these words, and that they were not spoken either by Euthydemus or Dionysodorus. I dare say, my good Crito, that they may have been spoken by some superior person: that I heard them I am certain.

CRITO:

Yes, indeed, Socrates, by some one a good deal superior, as I should be disposed to think. But did you carry the search any further, and did you find the art which you were seeking?

SOCRATES:

Find! my dear sir, no indeed. And we cut a poor figure; we were like children after larks, always on the point of catching the art, which was always getting away from us. But why should I repeat the whole story? At last we came to the kingly art, and enquired whether that gave and caused happiness, and then we got into a labyrinth, and when we thought we were at the end, came out again at the beginning, having still to seek as much as ever.

CRITO:

How did that happen, Socrates?

SOCRATES:

I will tell you; the kingly art was identified by us with the political.

CRITO:

Well, and what came of that?

SOCRATES:

To this royal or political art all the arts, including the art of the general, seemed to render up the supremacy, that being the only one which knew how to use what they produce. Here obviously was the very art which we were seeking—the art which is the source of good government, and which may be described, in the language of Aeschylus, as alone sitting at the helm of the vessel of state, piloting and governing all things, and utilizing them.

CRITO:

And were you not right, Socrates?

SOCRATES:

You shall judge, Crito, if you are willing to hear what followed; for we resumed the enquiry, and a question of this sort was asked: Does the kingly art, having this supreme authority, do anything for us? To be sure, was the answer. And would not you, Crito, say the same?

CRITO:

Yes, I should.

SOCRATES:

And what would you say that the kingly art does? If medicine were supposed to have supreme authority over the subordinate arts, and I were to ask you a similar question about that, you would say—it produces health?

CRITO:

I should.

SOCRATES:

And what of your own art of husbandry, supposing that to have supreme authority over the subject arts—what does that do? Does it not supply us with the fruits of the earth?

CRITO:

Yes.

SOCRATES:

And what does the kingly art do when invested with supreme power? Perhaps you may not be ready with an answer?

CRITO:

Indeed I am not, Socrates.

SOCRATES:

No more were we, Crito. But at any rate you know that if this is the art which we were seeking, it ought to be useful.

CRITO:

Certainly.

SOCRATES:

And surely it ought to do us some good?

CRITO:

Certainly, Socrates.

SOCRATES:

And Cleinias and I had arrived at the conclusion that knowledge of some kind is the only good.

CRITO:

Yes, that was what you were saying.

SOCRATES:

All the other results of politics, and they are many, as for example, wealth, freedom, tranquillity, were neither good nor evil in themselves; but the political science ought to make us wise, and impart knowledge to us, if that is the science which is likely to do us good, and make us happy.

CRITO:

Yes; that was the conclusion at which you had arrived, according to your report of the conversation.

SOCRATES:

And does the kingly art make men wise and good?

CRITO:

Why not, Socrates?

SOCRATES:

What, all men, and in every respect? and teach them all the arts,—carpentering, and cobbling, and the rest of them?

CRITO:

I think not, Socrates.

SOCRATES:

But then what is this knowledge, and what are we to do with it? For it is not the source of any works which are neither good nor evil, and gives no knowledge, but the knowledge of itself; what then can it be, and what are we to do with it? Shall we say, Crito, that it is the knowledge by which we are to make other men good?

CRITO:

By all means.

SOCRATES:

And in what will they be good and useful? Shall we repeat that they will make others good, and that these others will make others again, without ever determining in what they are to be good; for we have put aside the results of politics, as they are called. This is the old, old song over again; and we are just as far as ever, if not farther, from the knowledge of the art or science of happiness.

CRITO:

Indeed, Socrates, you do appear to have got into a great perplexity.

SOCRATES:

Thereupon, Crito, seeing that I was on the point of shipwreck, I lifted up my voice, and earnestly entreated and called upon the strangers to save me and the youth from the whirlpool of the argument; they were our Castor and Pollux, I said, and they should be serious, and show us in sober earnest what that knowledge was which would enable us to pass the rest of our lives in happiness.

CRITO:

And did Euthydemus show you this knowledge?

SOCRATES:

Yes, indeed; he proceeded in a lofty strain to the following effect: Would you rather, Socrates, said he, that I should show you this knowledge about which you have been doubting, or shall I prove that you already have it?

What, I said, are you blessed with such a power as this?

Indeed I am.

Then I would much rather that you should prove me to have such a knowledge; at my time of life that will be more agreeable than having to learn.

Then tell me, he said, do you know anything?

Yes, I said, I know many things, but not anything of much importance.

That will do, he said: And would you admit that anything is what it is, and at the same time is not what it is?

Certainly not.

And did you not say that you knew something?

I did.

If you know, you are knowing.

Certainly, of the knowledge which I have.

That makes no difference;—and must you not, if you are knowing, know all things?

Certainly not, I said, for there are many other things which I do not know.

And if you do not know, you are not knowing.

Yes, friend, of that which I do not know.

Still you are not knowing, and you said just now that you were knowing; and therefore you are and are not at the same time, and in reference to the same things.

A pretty clatter, as men say, Euthydemus, this of yours! and will you explain how I possess that knowledge for which we were seeking? Do you mean to say that the same thing cannot be and also not be; and therefore, since I know one thing, that I know all, for I cannot be knowing and not knowing at the same time, and if I know all things, then I must have the knowledge for which we are seeking—May I assume this to be your ingenious notion?

Out of your own mouth, Socrates, you are convicted, he said.

Well, but, Euthydemus, I said, has that never happened to you? for if I am only in the same case with you and our beloved Dionysodorus, I cannot complain. Tell me, then, you two, do you not know some things, and not know others?

Certainly not, Socrates, said Dionysodorus.

What do you mean, I said; do you know nothing?

Nay, he replied, we do know something.

Then, I said, you know all things, if you know anything?

Yes, all things, he said; and that is as true of you as of us.

O, indeed, I said, what a wonderful thing, and what a great blessing! And do all other men know all things or nothing?

Certainly, he replied; they cannot know some things, and not know others, and be at the same time knowing and not knowing.

Then what is the inference? I said.

They all know all things, he replied, if they know one thing.

O heavens, Dionysodorus, I said, I see now that you are in earnest; hardly have I got you to that point. And do you really and truly know all things, including carpentering and leather-cutting?

Certainly, he said.

And do you know stitching?

Yes, by the gods, we do, and cobbling, too.

And do you know things such as the numbers of the stars and of the sand?

Certainly; did you think we should say No to that?

By Zeus, said Ctesippus, interrupting, I only wish that you would give me some proof which would enable me to know whether you speak truly.

What proof shall I give you? he said.

Will you tell me how many teeth Euthydemus has? and Euthydemus shall tell how many teeth you have.

Will you not take our word that we know all things?

Certainly not, said Ctesippus: you must further tell us this one thing, and then we shall know that you are speak the truth; if you tell us the number, and we count them, and you are found to be right, we will believe the rest. They fancied that Ctesippus was making game of them, and they refused, and they would only say in answer to each of his questions, that they knew all things. For at last Ctesippus began to throw off all restraint; no question in fact was too bad for him; he would ask them if they knew the foulest things, and they, like wild boars, came rushing on his blows, and fearlessly replied that they did. At last, Crito, I too was carried away by my incredulity, and asked Euthydemus whether Dionysodorus could dance.

Certainly, he replied.

And can he vault among swords, and turn upon a wheel, at his age? has he got to such a height of skill as that?

He can do anything, he said.

And did you always know this?

Always, he said.

When you were children, and at your birth?

They both said that they did.

This we could not believe. And Euthydemus said: You are incredulous, Socrates.

Yes, I said, and I might well be incredulous, if I did not know you to be wise men.

But if you will answer, he said, I will make you confess to similar marvels.

Well, I said, there is nothing that I should like better than to be self-convicted of this, for if I am really a wise man, which I never knew before, and you will prove to me that I know and have always known all things, nothing in life would be a greater gain to me.

Answer then, he said.

Ask, I said, and I will answer.

Do you know something, Socrates, or nothing?

Something, I said.

And do you know with what you know, or with something else?

With what I know; and I suppose that you mean with my soul?

Are you not ashamed, Socrates, of asking a question when you are asked one?

Well, I said; but then what am I to do? for I will do whatever you bid; when I do not know what you are asking, you tell me to answer nevertheless, and not to ask again.

Why, you surely have some notion of my meaning, he said.

Yes, I replied.

Well, then, answer according to your notion of my meaning.

Yes, I said; but if the question which you ask in one sense is understood and answered by me in another, will that please you—if I answer what is not to the point?

That will please me very well; but will not please you equally well, as I imagine.

I certainly will not answer unless I understand you, I said.

You will not answer, he said, according to your view of the meaning, because you will be prating, and are an ancient.

Now I saw that he was getting angry with me for drawing distinctions, when he wanted to catch me in his springes of words. And I remembered that Connus was always angry with me when I opposed him, and then he neglected me, because he thought that I was stupid; and as I was intending to go to Euthydemus as a pupil, I reflected that I had better let him have his way, as he might think me a blockhead, and refuse to take me. So I said: You are a far better dialectician than myself, Euthydemus, for I have never made a profession of the art, and therefore do as you say; ask your questions once more, and I will answer.

Answer then, he said, again, whether you know what you know with something, or with nothing.

Yes, I said; I know with my soul.

The man will answer more than the question; for I did not ask you, he said, with what you know, but whether you know with something.

Again I replied, Through ignorance I have answered too much, but I hope that you will forgive me. And now I will answer simply that I always know what I know with something.

And is that something, he rejoined, always the same, or sometimes one thing, and sometimes another thing?

Always, I replied, when I know, I know with this.

Will you not cease adding to your answers?

My fear is that this word 'always' may get us into trouble.

You, perhaps, but certainly not us. And now answer: Do you always know with this?

Always; since I am required to withdraw the words 'when I know.'

You always know with this, or, always knowing, do you know some things with this, and some things with something else, or do you know all things with this?

All that I know, I replied, I know with this.

There again, Socrates, he said, the addition is superfluous.

Well, then, I said, I will take away the words 'that I know.'

Nay, take nothing away; I desire no favours of you; but let me ask: Would you be able to know all things, if you did not know all things?

Quite impossible.

And now, he said, you may add on whatever you like, for you confess that you know all things.

I suppose that is true, I said, if my qualification implied in the words 'that I know' is not allowed to stand; and so I do know all things.

And have you not admitted that you always know all things with that which you know, whether you make the addition of 'when you know them' or not? for you have acknowledged that you have always and at once known all things, that is to say, when you were a child, and at your birth, and when you were growing up, and before you were born, and before the heaven and earth existed, you knew all things, if you always know them; and I swear that you shall always continue to know all things, if I am of the mind to make you.

But I hope that you will be of that mind, reverend Euthydemus, I said, if you are really speaking the truth, and yet I a little doubt your power to make good your words unless you have the help of your brother Dionysodorus; then you may do it. Tell me now, both of you, for although in the main I cannot doubt that I really do know all things, when I am told so by men of your prodigious wisdom—how can I say that I know such things, Euthydemus, as that the good are unjust; come, do I know that or not?

Certainly, you know that.

What do I know?

That the good are not unjust.

Quite true, I said; and that I have always known; but the question is, where did I learn that the good are unjust?

Nowhere, said Dionysodorus.

Then, I said, I do not know this.

You are ruining the argument, said Euthydemus to Dionysodorus; he will be proved not to know, and then after all he will be knowing and not knowing at the same time.

Dionysodorus blushed.

I turned to the other, and said, What do you think, Euthydemus? Does not your omniscient brother appear to you to have made a mistake?

What, replied Dionysodorus in a moment; am I the brother of Euthydemus?

Thereupon I said, Please not to interrupt, my good friend, or prevent Euthydemus from proving to me that I know the good to be unjust; such a lesson you might at least allow me to learn.

You are running away, Socrates, said Dionysodorus, and refusing to answer.

No wonder, I said, for I am not a match for one of you, and a fortiori I must run away from two. I am no Heracles; and even Heracles could not fight against the Hydra, who was a she-Sophist, and had the wit to shoot up many new heads when one of them was cut off; especially when he saw a second monster of a sea-crab, who was also a Sophist, and appeared to have newly arrived from a sea-voyage, bearing down upon him from the left, opening his mouth and biting. When the monster was growing troublesome he called Iolaus, his nephew, to his help, who ably succoured him; but if my Iolaus, who is my brother Patrocles (the statuary), were to come, he would only make a bad business worse.

And now that you have delivered yourself of this strain, said Dionysodorus, will you inform me whether Iolaus was the nephew of Heracles any more than he is yours?

I suppose that I had best answer you, Dionysodorus, I said, for you will insist on asking—that I pretty well know—out of envy, in order to prevent me from learning the wisdom of Euthydemus.

Then answer me, he said.

Well then, I said, I can only reply that Iolaus was not my nephew at all, but the nephew of Heracles; and his father was not my brother Patrocles, but Iphicles, who has a name rather like his, and was the brother of Heracles.

And is Patrocles, he said, your brother?

Yes, I said, he is my half-brother, the son of my mother, but not of my father.

Then he is and is not your brother.

Not by the same father, my good man, I said, for Chaeredemus was his father, and mine was Sophroniscus.

And was Sophroniscus a father, and Chaeredemus also?

Yes, I said; the former was my father, and the latter his.

Then, he said, Chaeredemus is not a father.

He is not my father, I said.

But can a father be other than a father? or are you the same as a stone?

I certainly do not think that I am a stone, I said, though I am afraid that you may prove me to be one.

Are you not other than a stone?

I am.

And being other than a stone, you are not a stone; and being other than gold, you are not gold?

Very true.

And so Chaeredemus, he said, being other than a father, is not a father?

I suppose that he is not a father, I replied.

For if, said Euthydemus, taking up the argument, Chaeredemus is a father, then Sophroniscus, being other than a father, is not a father; and you, Socrates, are without a father.

Ctesippus, here taking up the argument, said: And is not your father in the same case, for he is other than my father?

Assuredly not, said Euthydemus.

Then he is the same?

He is the same.

I cannot say that I like the connection; but is he only my father, Euthydemus, or is he the father of all other men?

Of all other men, he replied. Do you suppose the same person to be a father and not a father?

Certainly, I did so imagine, said Ctesippus.

And do you suppose that gold is not gold, or that a man is not a man?

They are not 'in pari materia,' Euthydemus, said Ctesippus, and you had better take care, for it is monstrous to suppose that your father is the father of all.

But he is, he replied.

What, of men only, said Ctesippus, or of horses and of all other animals?

Of all, he said.

And your mother, too, is the mother of all?

Yes, our mother too.

Yes; and your mother has a progeny of sea-urchins then?

Yes; and yours, he said.

And gudgeons and puppies and pigs are your brothers?

And yours too.

And your papa is a dog?

And so is yours, he said.

If you will answer my questions, said Dionysodorus, I will soon extract the same admissions from you, Ctesippus. You say that you have a dog.

Yes, a villain of a one, said Ctesippus.

And he has puppies?

Yes, and they are very like himself.

And the dog is the father of them?

Yes, he said, I certainly saw him and the mother of the puppies come together.

And is he not yours?

To be sure he is.

Then he is a father, and he is yours; ergo, he is your father, and the puppies are your brothers.

Let me ask you one little question more, said Dionysodorus, quickly interposing, in order that Ctesippus might not get in his word: You beat this dog?

Ctesippus said, laughing, Indeed I do; and I only wish that I could beat you instead of him.

Then you beat your father, he said.

I should have far more reason to beat yours, said Ctesippus; what could he have been thinking of when he begat such wise sons? much good has this father of you and your brethren the puppies got out of this wisdom of yours.

But neither he nor you, Ctesippus, have any need of much good.

And have you no need, Euthydemus? he said.

Neither I nor any other man; for tell me now, Ctesippus, if you think it good or evil for a man who is sick to drink medicine when he wants it; or to go to war armed rather than unarmed.

Good, I say. And yet I know that I am going to be caught in one of your charming puzzles.

That, he replied, you will discover, if you answer; since you admit medicine to be good for a man to drink, when wanted, must it not be good for him to drink as much as possible; when he takes his medicine, a cartload of hellebore will not be too much for him?

Ctesippus said: Quite so, Euthydemus, that is to say, if he who drinks is as big as the statue of Delphi.

And seeing that in war to have arms is a good thing, he ought to have as many spears and shields as possible?

Very true, said Ctesippus; and do you think, Euthydemus, that he ought to have one shield only, and one spear?

I do.

And would you arm Geryon and Briareus in that way? Considering that you and your companion fight in armour, I thought that you would have known better...Here Euthydemus held his peace, but Dionysodorus returned to the previous answer of Ctesippus and said:—

Do you not think that the possession of gold is a good thing?

Yes, said Ctesippus, and the more the better.

And to have money everywhere and always is a good?

Certainly, a great good, he said.

And you admit gold to be a good?

Certainly, he replied.

And ought not a man then to have gold everywhere and always, and as much as possible in himself, and may he not be deemed the happiest of men who has three talents of gold in his belly, and a talent in his pate, and a stater of gold in either eye?

Yes, Euthydemus, said Ctesippus; and the Scythians reckon those who have gold in their own skulls to be the happiest and bravest of men (that is only another instance of your manner of speaking about the dog and father), and what is still more extraordinary, they drink out of their own skulls gilt, and see the inside of them, and hold their own head in their hands.

And do the Scythians and others see that which has the quality of vision, or that which has not? said Euthydemus.

That which has the quality of vision clearly.

And you also see that which has the quality of vision? he said. (Note: the ambiguity of (Greek), 'things visible and able to see,' (Greek), 'the speaking of the silent,' the silent denoting either the speaker or the subject of the speech, cannot be perfectly rendered in English. Compare Aristot. Soph. Elenchi (Poste's translation):—

'Of ambiguous propositions the following are instances:—

'I hope that you the enemy may slay.

'Whom one knows, he knows. Either the person knowing or the person known is here affirmed to know.

'What one sees, that one sees: one sees a pillar: ergo, that one pillar sees.

'What you *are* holding, that you are: you are holding a stone: ergo, a stone you are.

'Is a speaking of the silent possible? "The silent" denotes either the speaker are the subject of speech.

'There are three kinds of ambiguity of term or proposition. The first is when there is an equal linguistic propriety in several interpretations; the second when one is improper but customary; the third when the ambiguity arises in the combination of elements that are in themselves unambiguous, as in "knowing letters." "Knowing" and "letters" are perhaps separately unambiguous, but in combination may imply either that the letters are known, or that they themselves have knowledge. Such are the modes in which propositions and terms may be ambiguous.'

Yes, I do.

Then do you see our garments?

Yes.

Then our garments have the quality of vision.

They can see to any extent, said Ctesippus.

What can they see?

Nothing; but you, my sweet man, may perhaps imagine that they do not see; and certainly, Euthydemus, you do seem to me to have been caught napping when you were not asleep, and that if it be possible to speak and say nothing—you are doing so.

And may there not be a silence of the speaker? said Dionysodorus.

Impossible, said Ctesippus.

Or a speaking of the silent?

That is still more impossible, he said.

But when you speak of stones, wood, iron bars, do you not speak of the silent?

Not when I pass a smithy; for then the iron bars make a tremendous noise and outcry if they are touched: so that here your wisdom is strangely mistaken; please, however, to tell me how you can be silent when speaking (I thought that Ctesippus was put upon his mettle because Cleinias was present).

When you are silent, said Euthydemus, is there not a silence of all things?

Yes, he said.

But if speaking things are included in all things, then the speaking are silent.

What, said Ctesippus; then all things are not silent?

Certainly not, said Euthydemus.

Then, my good friend, do they all speak?

Yes; those which speak.

Nay, said Ctesippus, but the question which I ask is whether all things are silent or speak?

Neither and both, said Dionysodorus, quickly interposing; I am sure that you will be 'non-plussed' at that answer.

Here Ctesippus, as his manner was, burst into a roar of laughter; he said, That brother of yours, Euthydemus, has got into a dilemma; all is over with him. This delighted Cleinias, whose laughter made Ctesippus ten times as uproarious; but I cannot help thinking that the rogue must have picked up this answer from them; for there has been no wisdom like theirs in our time. Why do you laugh, Cleinias, I said, at such solemn and beautiful things?

Why, Socrates, said Dionysodorus, did you ever see a beautiful thing?

Yes, Dionysodorus, I replied, I have seen many.

Were they other than the beautiful, or the same as the beautiful?

Now I was in a great quandary at having to answer this question, and I thought that I was rightly served for having opened my mouth at all: I said however, They are not the same as absolute beauty, but they have beauty present with each of them.

And are you an ox because an ox is present with you, or are you Dionysodorus, because Dionysodorus is present with you?

God forbid, I replied.

But how, he said, by reason of one thing being present with another, will one thing be another?

Is that your difficulty? I said. For I was beginning to imitate their skill, on which my heart was set.

Of course, he replied, I and all the world are in a difficulty about the non-existent.

What do you mean, Dionysodorus? I said. Is not the honourable honourable and the base base?

That, he said, is as I please.

And do you please?

Yes, he said.

And you will admit that the same is the same, and the other other; for surely the other is not the same; I should imagine that even a child will hardly deny the other to be other. But I think, Dionysodorus, that you must have intentionally missed the last question; for in general you and your brother seem to me to be good workmen in your own department, and to do the dialectician's business excellently well.

What, said he, is the business of a good workman? tell me, in the first place, whose business is hammering?

The smith's.

And whose the making of pots?

The potter's.

And who has to kill and skin and mince and boil and roast?

The cook, I said.

And if a man does his business he does rightly?

Certainly.

And the business of the cook is to cut up and skin; you have admitted that?

Yes, I have admitted that, but you must not be too hard upon me.

Then if some one were to kill, mince, boil, roast the cook, he would do his business, and if he were to hammer the smith, and make a pot of the potter, he would do their business.

Poseidon, I said, this is the crown of wisdom; can I ever hope to have such wisdom of my own?

And would you be able, Socrates, to recognize this wisdom when it has become your own?

Certainly, I said, if you will allow me.

What, he said, do you think that you know what is your own?

Yes, I do, subject to your correction; for you are the bottom, and Euthydemus is the top, of all my wisdom.

Is not that which you would deem your own, he said, that which you have in your own power, and which you are able to use as you would desire, for example, an ox or a sheep—would you not think that which you could sell and give and sacrifice to any god whom you pleased, to be your own, and that which you could not give or sell or sacrifice you would think not to be in your own power?

Yes, I said (for I was certain that something good would come out of the questions, which I was impatient to hear); yes, such things, and such things only are mine.

Yes, he said, and you would mean by animals living beings?

Yes, I said.

You agree then, that those animals only are yours with which you have the power to do all these things which I was just naming?

I agree.

Then, after a pause, in which he seemed to be lost in the contemplation of something great, he said: Tell me, Socrates, have you an ancestral Zeus? Here, anticipating the final move, like a person caught in a net, who gives a desperate twist that he may get away, I said: No, Dionysodorus, I have not.

What a miserable man you must be then, he said; you are not an Athenian at all if you have no ancestral gods or temples, or any other mark of gentility.

Nay, Dionysodorus, I said, do not be rough; good words, if you please; in the way of religion I have altars and temples, domestic and ancestral, and all that other Athenians have.

And have not other Athenians, he said, an ancestral Zeus?

That name, I said, is not to be found among the Ionians, whether colonists or citizens of Athens; an ancestral Apollo there is, who is the father of Ion, and a family Zeus, and a Zeus guardian of the phratry, and an Athene guardian of the phratry. But the name of ancestral Zeus is unknown to us.

No matter, said Dionysodorus, for you admit that you have Apollo, Zeus, and Athene.

Certainly, I said.

And they are your gods, he said.

Yes, I said, my lords and ancestors.

At any rate they are yours, he said, did you not admit that?

I did, I said; what is going to happen to me?

And are not these gods animals? for you admit that all things which have life are animals; and have not these gods life?

They have life, I said.

Then are they not animals?

They are animals, I said.

And you admitted that of animals those are yours which you could give away or sell or offer in sacrifice, as you pleased?

I did admit that, Euthydemus, and I have no way of escape.

Well then, said he, if you admit that Zeus and the other gods are yours, can you sell them or give them away or do what you will with them, as you would with other animals?

At this I was quite struck dumb, Crito, and lay prostrate. Ctesippus came to the rescue.

Bravo, Heracles, brave words, said he.

Bravo Heracles, or is Heracles a Bravo? said Dionysodorus.

Poseidon, said Ctesippus, what awful distinctions. I will have no more of them; the pair are invincible.

Then, my dear Crito, there was universal applause of the speakers and their words, and what with laughing and clapping of hands and rejoicings the two men were quite overpowered; for hitherto their partisans only had cheered at each successive hit, but now the whole company shouted with delight until the columns of the Lyceum returned the sound, seeming to sympathize in their joy. To such a pitch was I affected myself, that I made a speech, in which I acknowledged that I had never seen the like of their wisdom; I was their devoted servant, and fell to praising and admiring of them. What marvellous dexterity of wit, I said, enabled you to acquire this great perfection in such a short time? There is much, indeed, to admire in your words, Euthydemus and Dionysodorus, but there is nothing that I admire more than your magnanimous disregard of any opinion—whether of the many, or of the grave and reverend seigniors—you regard only those who are like yourselves. And I do verily believe that there are few who are like you, and who would approve of such arguments; the majority of mankind are so ignorant of their value, that they would be more ashamed of employing them in the refutation of others than of being refuted by them. I must further express my approval of your kind and public-spirited denial of all differences, whether of good and evil, white or black, or any other; the result of which is that, as you say, every mouth is sewn up, not excepting your own, which graciously follows the example of others; and thus all ground of offence is taken away. But what appears to me to be more than all is, that this art and invention of yours has been so admirably contrived by you, that in a very short time it can be imparted to any one. I observed that Ctesippus learned to imitate you in no time. Now this quickness of attainment is an excellent thing; but at the same time I would advise you not to have any more public entertainments; there is a danger that men may undervalue an art which they have so easy an opportunity of acquiring; the exhibition would be best of all, if the discussion were confined to your two selves; but if there must be an audience, let him only be present who is willing to pay a handsome fee;—you should be careful of this;—and if you are wise, you will also bid your disciples discourse with no man but you and themselves. For only what is rare is valuable; and 'water,' which, as Pindar says, is the 'best of all things,' is also the cheapest. And now I have only to request that you will receive Cleinias and me among your pupils.

Such was the discussion, Crito; and after a few more words had passed between us we went away. I hope that you will come to them with me, since they say that they are able to teach any one who will give them money; no age or want of capacity is an impediment. And I must repeat one thing which they said, for your especial benefit,—that the learning of their art did not at all interfere with the business of money-making.

CRITO:

Truly, Socrates, though I am curious and ready to learn, yet I fear that I am not like-minded with Euthydemus, but one of the other sort, who, as you were saying, would rather be refuted by such arguments than use them in refutation of others. And though I may appear ridiculous in venturing to advise you, I think that you may as well hear what was said to me by a man of very considerable pretensions—he was a professor of legal oratory— who came away from you while I was walking up and down. 'Crito,' said he to me, 'are you giving no attention to these wise men?' 'No, indeed,' I said to him; 'I could not get within hearing of them—there was such a crowd.' 'You would have heard something worth hearing if you had.' 'What was that?' I said. 'You would have heard the greatest masters of the art of rhetoric discoursing.' 'And what did you think of them?' I said. 'What did I think of them?' he said:— 'theirs was the sort of discourse which anybody might hear from men who were playing the fool, and making much ado about nothing.' That was the expression which he used. 'Surely,' I said, 'philosophy is a charming thing.' 'Charming!' he said; 'what simplicity! philosophy is nought; and I think that if you had been present you would have been ashamed of your friend—his conduct was so very strange in placing himself at the mercy of men who care not what they say, and fasten upon every word. And these, as I was telling you, are supposed to be the most eminent professors of their time. But the truth is, Crito, that the study itself and the men themselves are utterly mean and ridiculous.' Now censure of the pursuit, Socrates, whether coming from him or from others, appears to me to be undeserved; but as to the impropriety of holding a public discussion with such men, there, I confess that, in my opinion, he was in the right.

SOCRATES:

O Crito, they are marvellous men; but what was I going to say? First of all let me know;—What manner of man was he who came up to you and censured philosophy; was he an orator who himself practises in the courts, or an instructor of orators, who makes the speeches with which they do battle?

CRITO:

He was certainly not an orator, and I doubt whether he had ever been into court; but they say that he knows the business, and is a clever man, and composes wonderful speeches.

SOCRATES:

Now I understand, Crito; he is one of an amphibious class, whom I was on the point of mentioning—one of those whom Prodicus describes as on the border-ground between philosophers and statesmen—they think that they are the wisest of all men, and that they are generally esteemed the wisest; nothing but the rivalry of the philosophers stands in their way; and they are of the opinion that if they can prove the philosophers to be good for nothing, no one will dispute their title to the palm of wisdom, for that they are themselves really the wisest, although they are apt to be mauled by Euthydemus and his friends, when they get hold of them in conversation. This opinion which they entertain of their own wisdom is very natural; for they have a certain amount of philosophy, and a certain amount of political wisdom; there is reason in what they say, for they argue that they have just enough of both, and so they keep out of the way of all risks and conflicts and reap the fruits of their wisdom.

CRITO:

What do you say of them, Socrates? There is certainly something specious in that notion of theirs.

SOCRATES:

Yes, Crito, there is more speciousness than truth; they cannot be made to understand the nature of intermediates. For all persons or things, which are intermediate between two other things, and participate in both of them—if one of these two things is good and the other evil, are better than the one and worse than the other; but if they are in a mean between two good things which do not tend to the same end, they fall short of either of their component elements in the attainment of their ends. Only in the case when the two component elements which do not tend to the same end are evil is the participant better than either. Now, if philosophy and political action are both good, but tend to different ends, and they participate in both, and are in a mean between them, then they are talking nonsense, for they are worse than either; or, if the one be good and the other evil, they are better than the one and worse than the other; only on the supposition that they are both evil could there be any truth in what they say. I do not think that they will admit that their two pursuits are either wholly or partly evil; but the truth is, that these philosopher-politicians who aim at both fall short of both in the attainment of their respective ends, and are really third, although they would like to stand first. There is no need, however, to be angry at this ambition of theirs— which may be forgiven; for every man ought to be loved who says and manfully pursues and works out anything which is at all like wisdom: at the same time we shall do well to see them as they really are.

CRITO:

I have often told you, Socrates, that I am in a constant difficulty about my two sons. What am I to do with them? There is no hurry about the younger one, who is only a child; but the other, Critobulus, is getting on, and needs some one who will improve him. I cannot help thinking, when I hear you talk, that there is a sort of madness in many of our anxieties about our children:—in the first place, about marrying a wife of good family to be the mother of them, and then about heaping up money for them— and yet taking no care about their education. But then again, when I contemplate any of those who pretend to educate others, I am amazed. To me, if I am to confess the truth, they all seem to be such outrageous beings: so that I do not know how I can advise the youth to study philosophy.

SOCRATES:

Dear Crito, do you not know that in every profession the inferior sort are numerous and good for nothing, and the good are few and beyond all price: for example, are not gymnastic and rhetoric and money-making and the art of the general, noble arts?

CRITO:

Certainly they are, in my judgment.

SOCRATES:

Well, and do you not see that in each of these arts the many are ridiculous performers?

CRITO:

Yes, indeed, that is very true.

SOCRATES:

And will you on this account shun all these pursuits yourself and refuse to allow them to your son?

CRITO:

That would not be reasonable, Socrates.

SOCRATES:

Do you then be reasonable, Crito, and do not mind whether the teachers of philosophy are good or bad, but think only of philosophy herself. Try and examine her well and truly, and if she be evil seek to turn away all men from her, and not your sons only; but if she be what I believe that she is, then follow her and serve her, you and your house, as the saying is, and be of good cheer.

CPSIA information can be obtained at www.ICGtesting.com
Printed in the USA
LVOW091023160911

246471LV00002B/239/P